PATCHES
DISCOVERY ADVENTURES

Copyrighted @ 2014 by Vincent R Faulkner

All rights reserved. No part or portion of this publication or any portion of images or stories may be reproduced, electronically or mechanically transferred in any form or fashion such as print, media, digital, physical products, stored in a retrieval systems, transmitted or used in any form or manner whatsoever without the exclusive express written legal permission of the author and publisher with the exception of the use of brief quotations or images in a book review or for promotions.

Created 2009
Printed in U.S.A
1ST Edition Printing 2014
All Content By Author

HONORABLE MENTION

And you may contribute a verse
What will your verse be?

No Matter what people tell you,
Words and ideas can change the World!

FAULKNER PUBLISHING -The Legacy Continues
Vincent R Faulkner
Smyrna, Tennessee 37167

Additional Copies:
PATCHESDISCOVERYADVENTURES.COM
EBOOKSBYFAULKNER.COM
Or AMAZON.COM

DEDICATION

This book is dedicated to the memory of our family pet Patches the dog. Patches impacted our lives so much during our time with her.

The characters in this book are real. They are my grandson Bubba (Peyton) and my granddaughter Bailee along with Patches the dog. These stories were created based on our family values and how Patches became a big part of them as all of us continued to grow in life together.

Who knew so much love could come from a free dog at Walmart on Thanksgiving Day! She kept giving us joy her entire life with us. Therefore her character has now been created to share with other children in hopes they will get as much joy from Patches travels through Patches Discovery Adventures with her.

Patches Discovery Adventures takes your child through adventures of everyday life lessons told in a very unique fun way. Everything is backed by biblical principles and includes memory map quests!

You can have tons of enjoyment for you and your child in the simplest form of just reading and sharing pictures with your little ones with audio books to match each journey. While teaching them all the important things you want them to know in life in a fun exciting way for them.

From our family to yours we hope you enjoy and share Patches Discovery Adventures with every child you know to give them a great start at becoming all they can be in life through sound solid life principles and values.

Everyone Meet PATCHES!

PATCHES is a very special dog. She has all these different patches of hair that make up her coat of characters. Her character patches are what make **PATCHES** who she is. Just like your character makes you who you are!

PATCHES has something incredible about her! When she is on her DISCOVERY ADVENTURE JOURNEYS the different character patches on her hair FLASH to teach her the right thing to do every where she goes! WOOF! Come and join PATCHES as she starts TRAVELING on her EXCITING DISCOVERY ADVENTURE JOURNEYS

PATCHES
DISCOVERY ADVENTURES

03

Let's begin PATCHES DISCOVERY ADVENTURES TRAVEL QUEST JOURNEYS that takes us too:

04 PATCHES HONESTY DISCOVERY ADVENTURE
06 PATCHES FORGIVE DISCOVERY ADVENTURE
08 PATCHES NEVER GIVE UP DISCOVERY ADVENTURE
15 PATCHES HAPPY DISCOVERY ADVENTURE
17 PATCHES HEALTHY DISCOVERY ADVENTURE
19 PATCHES LEARNING DISCOVERY ADVENTURE
26 PATCHES COURAGE DISCOVERY ADVENTURE
28 PATCHES RESPECT DISCOVERY ADVENTURE
30 PATCHES SHARING DISCOVERY ADVENTURE

PATCHES TRAVEL QUEST JOURNEY ONE STARTS NOW!

PATCHES HONESTY DISCOVERY ADVENTURE!

PATCHES, BUBBA and BAILEE are walking through the park and see children playing soccer.

BUBBA sees that a little boy dropped a dollar out of his pocket playing soccer.

PATCHES, character question for you is,

Should PATCHES, BUBBA and BAILEE tell the little boy he dropped his dollar or keep it?

PATCH HILLS PLAY PARK

LET'S SEE HOW PATCHES, BUBBA AND BAILEE SOLVE PATCHES HONESTY DISCOVERY ADVENTURE!

BUBBA SAYS: The little boy dropped a dollar playing soccer. What should we do?

BAILEE SAYS: PATCHES has a YELLOW PATCH FLASHING HONESTY on her coat!
Can you see the YELLOW PATCH FLASHING HONESTY?
PATCHES, what is the YELLOW PATCH FLASHING HONESTY telling us to do?

PATCHES BARKS: ARF! ARF! Tell the truth about everything and give the dollar to the boy. WOOF! Always be HONEST to everyone Be an HONEST person!

PATCH HILLS PLAY PARK

ISAIAH 26:3 The king is pleased \with words from righteous lips; he loves those who speak honestly

PATCHES NEXT TRAVEL QUEST ON JOURNEY ONE IS TAKING US TO PATCHES FORGIVE DISCOVERY ADVENTURE!

06

PATCHES FORGIVE DISCOVERY ADVENTURE!

PATCHES, BUBBA and BAILEE are at home talking about their Mom's birthday yesterday. BAILEE notices their Dad is saying I am sorry to their Mom for missing her birthday when he went fishing yesterday.

But, BAILEE,, BUBBA and PATCHES can't tell whether Mom will FORGIVE Dad for his mistake and accept his apology or not?.

PATCHES, character question for you is,

Should PATCHES, BUBBA and BAILEE accept apologies for a mistake and FORGIVE people or not?!

I will not accept your apology and never forgive you
OR
I will accept your apology and always forgive you

I am sorry
I missed
You're birthday

LET'S SEE HOW PATCHES, BUBBA AND BAILEE SOLVE PATCHES FORGIVE DISCOVERY ADVENTURE

BAILEE SAYS: Mom does not know if she will FORGIVE Dad for making a mistake and missing her birthday yesterday.. Should we FORGIVE or not FORGIVE someone for making a mistake?

BUBBA SAYS: PATCHES has a YELLOW PATCH FLASHING FORGIVE on her coat! Can you see the YELLOW PATCH FLASHING FORGIVE? PATCHES what is the YELLOW PATCH FLASHING FORGIVE telling us to do?

PATCHES BARKS: ARF! ARF! Always FORGIVE everyone for making a mistake just as You would want someone to FORGIVE you for the mistakes that you make.

BAILEE SAYS: What BIBLE VERSE teaches us about FORGIVENESS?

Please forgive me

I will accept your apology and always forgive you

I am sorry I missed your birthday

FORGIVE

COLOSSIANS 3:13 Bear with one another, and forgiving each other. If any man has a complaint against any, even as Christ forgave you, so you do.

PATCHES NEXT TRAVEL QUEST JOURNEY ONE IS TAKING US TO PATCHES NEVER GIVE UP DISCOVERY ADVENTURE

PATCHES NEVER GIVE UP DISCOVERY ADVENTURE

PATCHES, BUBBA and BAILEE are at school watching kids running in a race.

BUBBA notices that a little boy quit running
He is walking and giving up because he did not win the race.

PATCHES character question for you is.

Should PATCHES, BUBBA and BAILEE give up and quit if they

PATCHVILLE RACE TODAY!

LET'S SEE HOW PATCHES, BUBBA AND BAILEE SOLVE PATCHES NEVER GIVE UP DISCOVERY ADVENTURE!

BAILEE SAYS: The boy did not win the race so he is walking and giving up. Should we give up and quit if we don't win a race too?

BUBBA SAYS: PATCHES has a YELLOW PATCH FLASHING NEVER GIVE UP on her coat!
Can you see the YELLOW PATCH FLASHING NEVER GIVE UP?
PATCHES what is the YELLOW PATCH FLASHING NEVER GIVE UP patch telling us to do?

PATCHES BARKS: ARF! ARF! Never quit anything!
Always finish what you start and NEVER GIVE UP!
Be a person who NEVER GIVES UP!
What kind of person should you be?

BUBBA SAYS: What BIBLE VERSE teaches us about NEVER GIVING UP?

'2' CHRONICLES 15:7 But as for you, be strong and do not give up, for your work will be rewarded

PATCHES NEXT TRAVEL QUEST ON JOURNEY ONE IS TAKING US TO THE PATCHES MEMORY DISCOVERY ADVENTURE

BUBBA SAYS: We have TRAVELED through '3' EXCITING PATCHES DISCOVERY ADVENTURES on this JOURNEY!

BAILEE SAYS: We are having so much fun on our DISCOVERY ADVENTURES!!

What has this JOURNEY taught us TRAVELING through PATCHES EXCITING DISCOVERY ADVENTURES?

PATCHES BARKS: ARF! ARF, Let's remember the '3' PATCHES DISCOVERY ADVENTURES together!

PATCHES HONESTY DISCOVERY ADVENTURE
Always be HONEST and tell the truth to everyone about everything. Be an HONEST person. WOOF!

PATCHES FORGIVE DISCOVERY ADVENTURE
Always FORGIVE everyone for making a mistake, as you would want to be FORGIVEN for your mistakes.
Be a person who will FORGIVE someone WOOF! WOOF!

PATCHES NEVER GIVE UP DISCOVERY ADVENTURE
Never quit anything! Always finish what you start and NEVER GIVE UP. Be a person who NEVER GIVES UP!

PATCHES NEXT TRAVEL QUEST ON JOURNEY ONE IS TAKING US TO PATCHES BIBLE MEMORY DISCOVERY ADVENTURE!

BUBBA SAYS: We have TRAVELED through '3' EXCITING PATCHES BIBLE DISCOVERY ADVENTURES on this JOURNEY!

BAILEE SAYS: We are having so much fun on PATCHES BIBLE DISCOVERY ADVENTURES too!

PATCHES BARKS: ARF! ARF! Let's remember the '3' PATCHES BIBLE DISCOVERY ADVENTURES together?

OUR '3' PATCHES BIBLE DISCOVERY ADVENTURES WERE:

PATCHES HONESTY BIBLE DISCOVERY ADVENTURE
The king is pleased with words from righteous lips; he loves those Who speak honestly. ISAIAH 26:3 WOOF!

PATCHES FORGIVE BIBLE DISCOVERY ADVENTURE
Bear with one another, and forgiving each other, If any man has a Complaint against any, even as Christ forgave you, so you also do. COLOSSIANS 3:13 ARF! ARF!

PATCHES NEVER GIVE UP BIBLE DISCOVERY ADVENTURE
But as for you, be strong and do not give up, for your work will be rewarded '2' CHRONICLES 15:7

PATCHES NEXT TRAVEL QUEST ON JOURNEY ONE IS TAKING US TOO

PATCHES DISCOVERY ADVENTURES
MEMORY MAP QUEST ONE

BUBBA SAYS: We have TRAVELED through '3' EXCITING PATCHES BIBLE DISCOVERY ADVENTURES. What BIBLE VERSES did we learn about on this JOURNEY?

PATCHES BARKS: ARF! ARF! Our TRAVEL QUEST on JOURNEY ONE takes us to PATCHES DISCOVERY ADVENTURES MEMORY MAP QUEST ONE! Let's get started and use our memory together! WOOF! Fill in the missing words as we TRAVEL back through PATCHES DISCOVERY ADVENTURES JOURNEY ONE together.!

If you tell the truth you are an HONEST person. If you tell the truth you are a _____ person. The missing word is HONEST WOOF!

ISAIAH 26:3 SAYS: The king is pleased with words from righteous lips; he loves those who speak HONESTLY. The king is pleased with words from righteous lips; he loves those who speak _____. The missing word in HONESTLY!

Always FORGIVE everyone for mistakes, as you would want to be forgiven when you make a mistake Always _____ everyone for mistakes, as you would want to be forgiven when you make a mistake. The missing word is FORGIVE!

COLOSSIANS 3:13 SAYS: Bear with one another, and FORGIVE each other.
Bear with one another, and _____ each other.
The missing word is FORGIVE! WOOF!

Always complete everything you start and NEVER GIVE UP!.
Always complete everything you start and _____.
The missing words are NEVER GIVE UP! ARF! ARF!

2' CHRONICLES 15:7 SAYS: But as for you, be strong and NEVER GIVE UP, for your work will be rewarded But as for you, be strong and _____, for your work will be rewarded The missing words are NEVER GIVE UP!

WOOF! Great Job!

You have just earned PATCHES PIONEER PAW BADGE ONE! When you finish all '3' TRAVEL QUEST JOURNEYS with all '9' PATCHES DISCOVERY ADVENTURES

You can become a JUNIOR EXPLORER in PATCHES DISCOVERY ADVENTURES PAW PATROL! ARF! ARF!

ARF! ARF! Remember to practice what You learn on PATCHES DISCOVERY ADVENTURE TRAVEL QUEST JOURNEYS!

It makes you a better you! WOOF!

You are now ready for more EXCITING PATCHES DISCOVERY ADVENTURES with PATCHES DISCOVERY ADVENTURES TRAVEL QUEST JOURNEY TWO!

PATCHES
DISCOVERY ADVENTURES

Let's begin PATCHES DISCOVERY ADVENTURES TRAVEL QUEST JOURNEY TWO that takes us too:

04 PATCHES HAPPY DISCOVERY ADVENTURE

06 PATCHES HEALTHY DISCOVERY ADVENTURE

08 PATCHES LEARNING DISCOVERY ADVENTURE

10 PATCHES MEMORY DISCOVERY ADVENTURE

11 PATCHES BIBLE MEMORY DISCOVERY ADVENTURE

12 PATCHES MEMORY MAP QUEST JOURNEY ONE

PATCHES TRAVEL QUEST DISCOVERY ADVENTURES JOURNEY TWO STARTS NOW!

PATCHES HAPPY DISCOVERY ADVENTURE!

PATCHES, BUBBA and BAILEE are walking in the park on a SUNNY day.

BAILEE notices a little boy is very angry and a little girl is very HAPPY.

PATCHES, character question for you is,

Should PATCHES, BUBBA and BAILEE be angry or HAPPY?

PATCH HILLS PLAY PARK

LET'S SEE HOW PATCHES, BUBBA AND BAILEE SOLVE PATCHES HAPPY DISCOVERY ADVENTURE!

BAILEE SAYS: That little boy looks angry and the little girl looks HAPPY. Should we be angry or HAPPY?

BUBBA SAYS: PATCHES has a YELLOW PATCH FLASHING HAPPY on her coat!
Can you see the YELLOW PATCH FLASHING HAPPY?
PATCHES, what is the YELLOW PATCH FLASHING HAPPY telling us to do?

PATCHES BARKS: ARF! ARF! Always be HAPPY and do not be angry.
Being HAPPY makes you and others feel good!
Be a HAPPY person!
What type of person should you be?

BAILEE SAYS: What BIBLE VERSE teaches us about being HAPPY?

PSALM 68:3 But may the righteous be glad and rejoice before God; may they be happy and joyful.

PATCHES NEXT TRAVEL QUEST ON JOURNEY TWO IS TAKING US TO PATCHES HEALTHY DISCOVERY ADVENTURE

PATCHES HEALTHY DISCOVERY ADVENTURE

PATCHES, BUBBA and BAILEE are getting something to eat at a picnic.

BAILEE sees a little boy confused because there are so many things to eat. He does not know if he should eat HEALTHY good food or other food that may not be good for him.

PATCHES character question for you is.

Should PATCHES, BUBBA and BAILEE eat HEALTHY food or other food?

LET'S SEE HOW PATCHES, BUBBA AND BAILEE SOLVE PATCHES HEALTHY DISCOVERY ADVENTURE

BAILEE SAYS: The little boy is confused about whether to eat food that is good for him or food that may not be good for him. Should we eat food that is good for us or for that may not be good for us?

BUBBA SAYS: PATCHES has a YELLOW PATCH FLASHING HEALTHY on her coat! Can you see the YELLOW PATCH FLASHING HEALTHY? PATCHES, what is the YELLOW PATCH FLASHING HEALTHY telling us to do?

PATCHES BARKS: WOOF! Always eat 'good' food like fruit, vegetables and drink milk and juice to grow strong and smart. Be a HEALTHY person! What type of person should you be?

BAILEE SAYS: What BIBLE VERSE teaches us about being HEALTHY?

JOHN 3 – 1:2 Beloved, I pray that all may go well with you and that you may be in good HEALTH, as it goes well with your soul.

PATCHES NEXT TRAVEL QUEST ON JOURNEY TWO IS TAKING US TO PATCHES LEARNING DISCOVERY ADVENTURE!

PATCHES LEARNING DISCOVERY ADVENTURE!

PATCHES, BUBBA and BAILEE are at school in their class LEARNING math.

BUBBA notices a little boy is daydreaming and not paying attention to LEARN the math.

PATCHES character question for you is.

Should PATCHES, BUBBA and BAILEE daydream and not pay attention so they do not LEARN math in class too?

LET'S SEE HOW PATCHES, BUBBA AND BAILEE SOLVE PATCHES LEARNING DISCOVERY ADVENTURE!

20

BAILEE SAYS: That boy is daydreaming and not paying attention to learn. Should we daydream and not pay attention so we do not learn in class too?

BUBBA SAYS: PATCHES has a YELLOW PATCH FLASHING learning on her coat! Can you see the YELLOW PATCH FLASHING learning? PATCHES, what is the YELLOW PATCH FLASHING learning patch telling us to do?

PATCHES barks, WOOF! LEARN something new everyday!
Never daydream or ignore someone teaching you.
Be a smart person and always pay attention to everyone.
Be a person who is always LEARNING!
What type of person should you be?

BAILEE SAYS: What BIBLE VERSE teaches us about LEARNING?

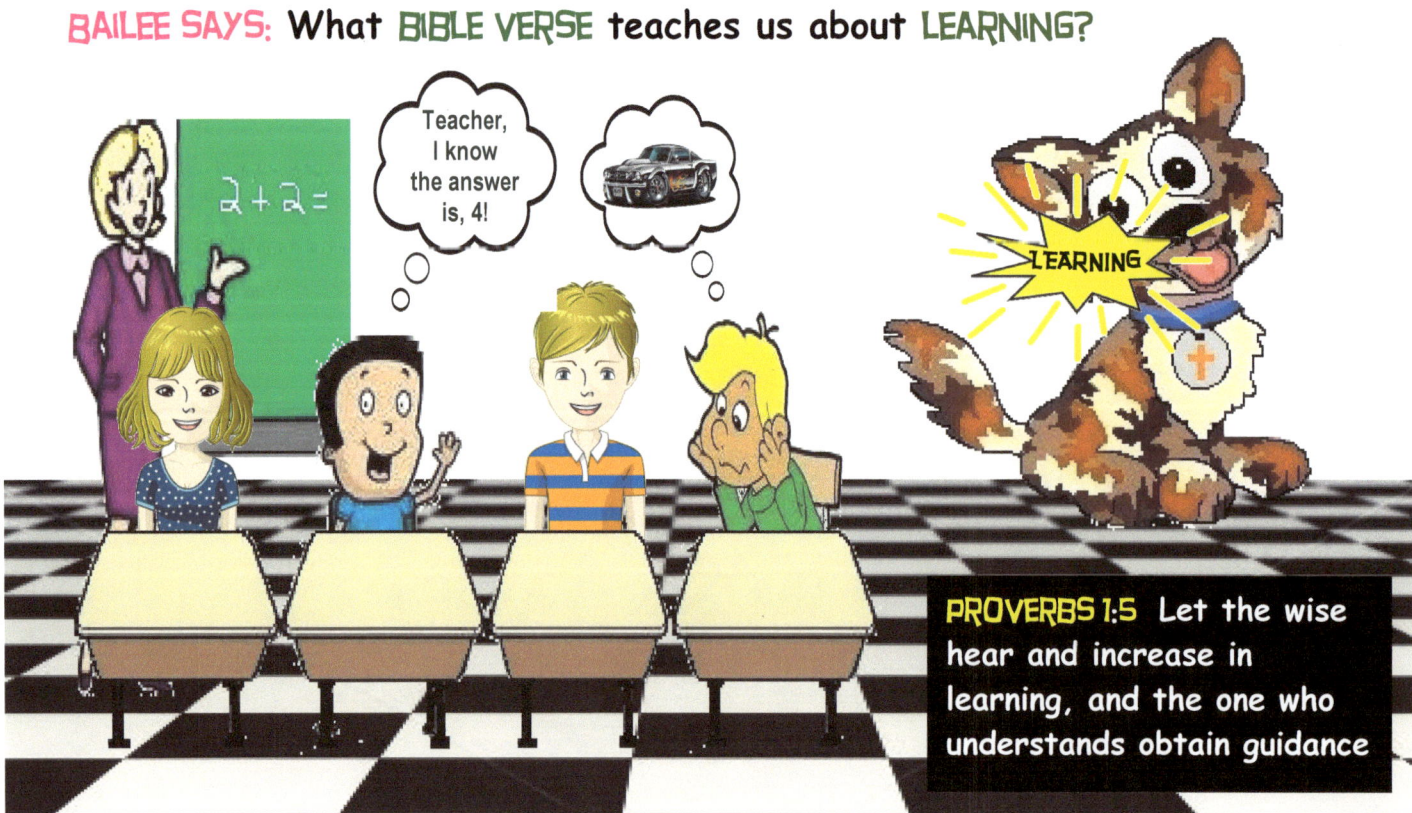

PROVERBS 1:5 Let the wise hear and increase in learning, and the one who understands obtain guidance

PATCHES NEXT TRAVEL QUEST ON JOURNEY TWO IS TAKING US TO PATCHES MEMORY DISCOVERY ADVENTURE

BUBBA SAYS: We have TRAVELED through '3' EXCITING PATCHES DISCOVERY ADVENTURES on this JOURNEY!

BAILEE SAYS: Patches, WOOF! We are having so much fun on our DISCOVERY ADVENTURES!
What has this JOURNEY taught us TRAVELING through PATCHES EXCITING DISCOVERY ADVENTURES?

PATCHES BARKS: Lets see what EXCITING ADVENTURES on PATCHES TRAVEL QUEST OURNEY TWO that you have completed

Can you remember the '3' PATCHES DISCOVERY ADVENTURES In TRAVEL QUEST JOURNEY TWO?

Lets remember the '3' PATCHES DISCOVERY ADVENTURES together!
WOOF! WOOF! Our '3' EXCITING PATCHES DISCOVERY ADVENTURES were:

PATCHES HAPPY DISCOVERY ADVENTURE
Always be HAPPY and do not be angry. Being HAPPY makes you and others feel good. Be a HAPPY person! WOOF!

PATCHES HEALTHY DISCOVERY ADVENTURE
Always eat 'good' food like fruit, vegetables and drink milk and juice to grow HEALTHY strong and smart. Be a HEALTHY person! ARF!

PATCHES LEARNING DISCOVERY ADVENTURE
Never daydream or ignore someone who is teaching you.
Be a person who is LEARNING something new everyday.
Be a person who is always LEARNING!
What kind of person should you be?

PATCHES NEXT TRAVEL QUEST ON JOURNEY TWO IS TAKING US TO PATCHES BIBLE MEMORY DISCOVERY ADVENTURE!

BUBBA SAYS: Patches, we have TRAVELED through '3' EXCITING PATCHES BIBLE DISCOVERY ADVENTURES on this JOURNEY!

BAILEE SAYS: PATCHES ARF! ARF! We are having so much fun on PATCHES BIBLE DISCOVERY ADVENTURES

BUBBA SAYS: What BIBLE VERSES did we LEARN about on this JOURNEY TRAVELING through PATCHES DISCOVERY ADVENTURES?

WOOF! Can you remember the '3' PATCHES BIBLE DISCOVERY ADVENTURES In TRAVEL QUEST JOURNEY TWO? ARF! ARF!

Lets remember the '3' PATCHES BIBLE DISCOVERY ADVENTURES together! Our '3' PATCHES BIBLE DISCOVERY ADVENTURES were:

PATCHES HAPPY BIBLE DISCOVERY ADVENTURE
But may the righteous be glad and rejoice before God; may they be HAPPY and joyful. PSALM 68:3 WOOF!

PATCHES HEALTHY BIBLE DISCOVERY ADVENTURE
Beloved, I pray that all may go well with you and that you may be in good in HEALTH, as it goes well with your soul. JOHN 3 – 1:2 ARF!

PATCHES LEARNING BIBLE DISCOVERY ADVENTURE
Let the wise hear and increase in LEARNING, and the one who Understand and obtains guidance PROVERBS 1:5

PATCHES DISCOVERY ADVENTURES
JOURNEYS MEMORY MAP QUEST TWO

BAILEE SAYS: PATCHES ARF! ARF! We are having so much fun traveling on our BIBLE DISCOVERY ADVENTURE too!
What has this JOURNEY taught us TRAVELING on PATCHES BIBLE DISCOVERY ADVENTURES?

PATCHES BARKS: WOOF! Our TRAVEL QUEST on JOURNEY TWO takes us to PATCHES DISCOVERY ADVENTURES MEMORY MAP QUEST TWO!
Let's get started and use our MEMORY together!
Fill in the missing words as we travel back through PATCHES DISCOVERY ADVENTURES JOURNEY TWO together.

Always be HAPPY and do not be angry. It makes you and others feel good inside. Always be _____ and do not be angry. It makes you and others feel good inside. The missing word is HAPPY!

PSALM 68:3 SAYS But, may the righteous be glad and rejoice before God; may they be HAPPY and joyful. But, may the righteous be glad and rejoice before God; may they be _____ and joyful. The missing word is HAPPY!

Always eat 'good' food like fruit, vegetables and drink milk and juice to grow HEALTHY strong and smart Always eat 'good' food like fruit, vegetables and drink milk and juice to grow _____, strong and smart.
The missing word is HEALTHY!

JOHN 3 – 1:2 SAYS: Beloved, I pray that all may go well with you and that you may be in good HEALTH, as it goes well with your soul. Beloved, I pray that all may go well with you and that you may be in _____, as it goes well with your soul. The missing words are GOOD HEALTH!

Never daydream or ignore someone who is teaching you. Be a person who is LEARNING something new everyday. Never daydream or ignore someone who is teaching you. Be a person who is _____ something new everyday.
The missing word is LEARNING!

PROVERBS 1:5 SAYS: Let the wise hear and increase in LEARNING and the one who understands obtain guidance. Let the wise hear and increase in_____, and the one who understands obtain guidance. The missing word is LEARNING!

WOOF! Great Job!

You have just earned PATCHES PIONEER PAW BADGE TWO!
When you finish all '3' TRAVEL QUEST JOURNEYS
with all '9' PATCHES DISCOVERY ADVENTURES
You can become a JUNIOR EXPLORER in
PATCHES DISCOVERY ADVENTURES PAW PATROL!

ARF! ARF! Remember, practice what you learn on PATCHES DISCOVERY ADVENTURE TRAVEL QUEST JOURNEYS!

It makes you a better you! WOOF!

You are now ready for more exciting PATCHES DISCOVERY ADVENTURES with PATCHES DISCOVERY ADVENTURES TRAVEL QUEST JOURNEY THREE!

PATCHES
DISCOVERY ADVENTURES

Let's begin PATCHES DISCOVERY ADVENTURES TRAVEL QUEST JOURNEY THREE that takes us too:

04 PATCHES COURAGE DISCOVERY ADVENTURE

06 PATCHES RESPECT DISCOVERY ADVENTURE

09 PATCHES SHARING DISCOVERY ADVENTURE

11 PATCHES MEMORY DISCOVERY ADVENTURE

12 PATCHES BIBLE MEMORY DISCOVERY ADVENTURE

13 PATCHES MEMORY MAP QUEST JOURNEY THREE

PATCHES TRAVEL QUEST DISCOVERY ADVENTURES JOURNEY THREE STARTS NOW!

PATCHES COURAGE DISCOVERY ADVENTURE!

PATCHES, BUBBA and BAILEE are watching boy scouts climb a big hill in the woods.

BAILEE notices a little boy is afraid that he can't make it climbing up the hill His friends are telling him to have courage and he can make it!

PATCHES, character question for you is.

Should PATCHES, BUBBA and BAILEE have courage to climb the hill or just quit because they don't believe they can climb the hill?

You can do it! Have courage and believe in yourself .We believe in you!

I am afraid that I can't make it up the hill.

PATCH HILLS CAMP GROUND

LET'S SEE HOW BUBBA, BAILEE AND PATCHES SOLVE PATCHES COURAGE DISCOVERY ADVENTURE!

BAILEE SAYS: The little boy is afraid to climb the hill. He has no courage and wants to give up and not try!.

BUBBA SAYS: PATCHES has a YELLOW PATCH FLASHING COURAGE on her coat! Can you see the YELLOW PATCH FLASHING COURAGE? PATCHES, what is the YELLOW PATCH FLASHING COURAGE telling us to do?

PATCHES barks: ARF! ARF! Always have courage and don't be afraid. Believe in yourself and you will be able to accomplish anything! Be a person with COURAGE! What kind of person should you be?

BAILEE SAYS: What BIBLE VERSE teaches us about COURAGE?

You can do it! Have courage and believe in yourself. We believe in you!

I will have courage and I can make it up the hill!

DEUTERONOMY 31:6 Be strong and courageous. Do not be afraid or terrified of them, for the Lord your God goes with you; he will never leave you nor forsake you.

PATCH HILLS CAMP GROUND

PATCHES NEXT TRAVEL QUEST ON JOURNEY THREE IS TAKING US TOO PATCHES RESPECT DISCOVERY ADVENTURE!

PATCHES RESPECT DISCOVERY ADVENTURE!

PATCHES, BUBBA and BAILEE went over to Tommy's house to play.

BUBBA notices Tommy is not speaking very nice to his Mother.

PATCHES character question for you is.

Should PATCHES, BUBBA and BAILEE not speak nice to their Mother

MOM, MOM, MOM
Come and change the TV channel for me now! Bring me something to eat and hurry up!

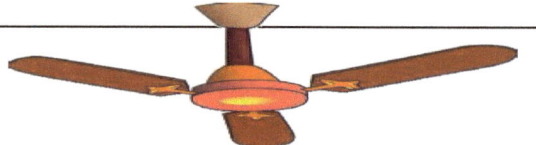

BEFORE WE START TO GAIN KNOWLEDGE WE OUGHT TO START WITH RESPECT FOR GOD

LET'S SEE HOW PATCHES, BAILEE AND BUBBA SOLVE PATCHES RESPECT DISCOVERY ADVENTURE

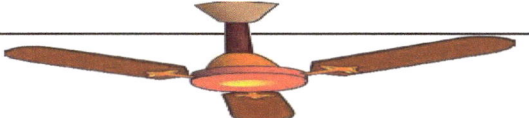

BUBBA SAYS: Tommy is not speaking very polite to his mother. He did not say please and was not being nice to his Mother.

BAILEE SAYS: PATCHES has a YELLOW PATCH FLASHING RESPECT on her coat!
Can you see the YELLOW PATCH FLASHING RESPECT?
PATCHES, what is the YELLOW PATCH FLASHING RESPECT telling us to do?

PATCHES BARKS, WOOF! Be nice and show respect to your parents!
Always say please and thank you
Be polite and respect everyone all the time!
Be a person who shows RESPECT to everyone
What type of person should you be?

BUBBA SAYS: What BIBLE VERSE teaches us about RESPECT?

MOM, MOM, MOM
May I please change the channel on the TV? Can I help you in the kitchen and have something to eat?

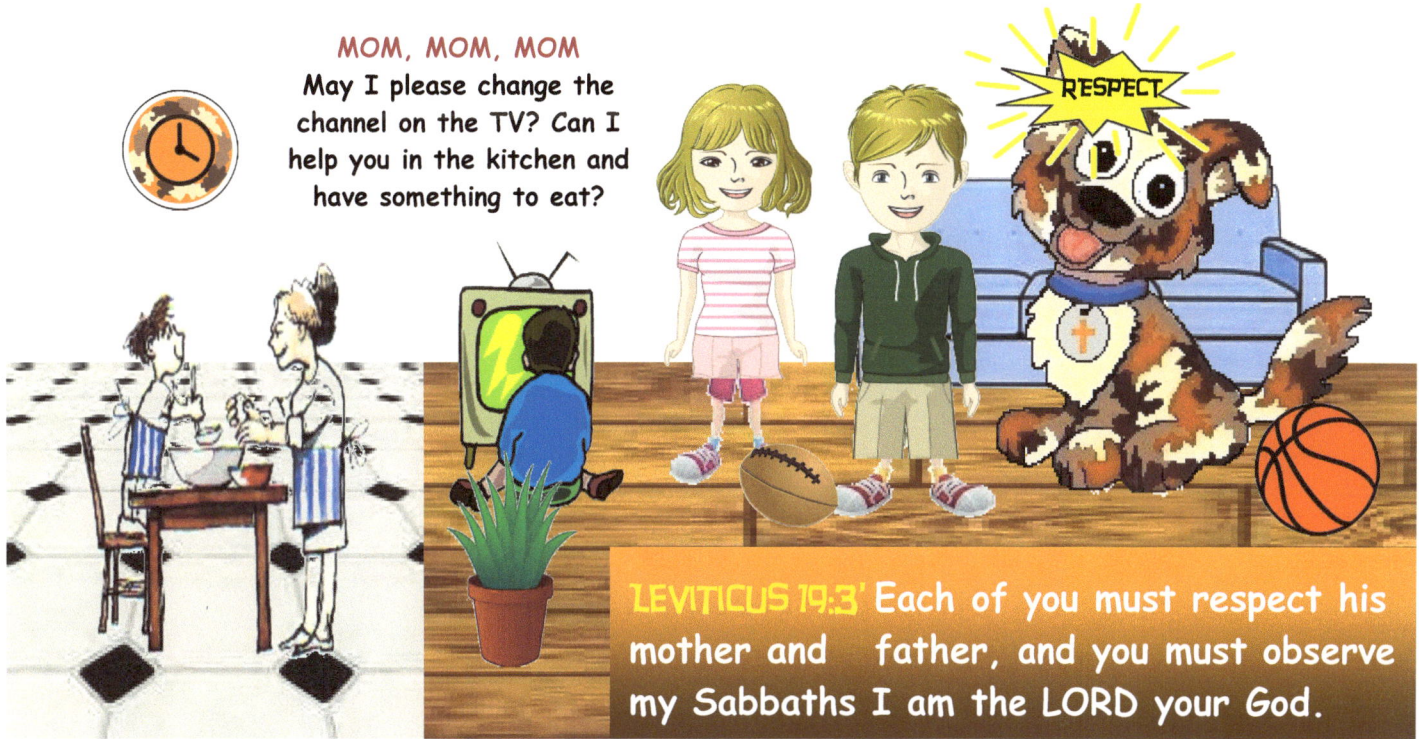

LEVITICUS 19:3 'Each of you must respect his mother and father, and you must observe my Sabbaths I am the LORD your God.

PATCHES NEXT TRAVEL QUEST ON JOURNEY THREE IS TAKING US TO PATCHES SHARING DISCOVERY ADVENTURE!

PATCHES SHARING DISCOVERY ADVENTURE!

PATCHES, BUBBA and BAILEE are at a party with friends playing outside.

BAILEE says oh no, a little boy is saying there is only one pizza for everyone to eat.

PATCHES character question for you is.

Should PATCHES, BUBBA and BAILEE eat the one pizza and not share with anyone else?

LET'S SEE HOW PATCHES, BAILEE AND BUBBA SOLVE PATCHES SHARING DISCOVERY ADVENTURE

BUBBA says: There is only one pizza for everyone to eat. How will all of the kids eat?

BAILEE says: PATCHES has a YELLOW PATCH FLASHING SHARE on her coat. Can you see the YELLOW PATCH FLASHING SHARE? PATCHES, what is the YELLOW PATCH FLASHING SHARE telling us to do?

PATCHES barks: ARF! ARF! It is polite to always 'SHARE' with others. Remember, if you 'SHARE' with someone then you 'care' for someone. What type of person should you be? Be a person who will SHARE with others!

HEBREWS 13:16 And do not forget do good and to share with others, for with such sacrifices God is pleased.

PATCHES NEXT TRAVEL QUEST ON JOURNEY THREE IS TAKING US TO PATCHES MEMORY DISCOVERY ADVENTURE

BUBBA SAYS: We have TRAVELED through '3' EXCITING PATCHES DISCOVERY ADVENTURES on this JOURNEY!

BAILEE SAYS: PATCHES, WOOF! We are having so much fun on our DISCOVERY ADVENTURES!

PATCHES BARKS: ARF, ARF! Let's see what EXCITING DISCOVERY ADVENTURES on PATCHES TRAVEL QUEST JOURNEY THREE that you have completed

Can you remember the '3' PATCHES DISCOVERY ADVENTURES In TRAVEL QUEST JOURNEY THREE?

Lets remember the '3' PATCHES DISCOVERY ADVENTURES together! Our '3' EXCITING PATCHES DISCOVERY ADVENTURES were:

PATCHES COURAGE DISCOVERY ADVENTURE
Always have COURAGE and don't be afraid. Believe in yourself and you can do anything! WOOF! WOOF!

PATCHES RESPECT DISCOVERY ADVENTURE
Be polite and show respect to your parents and others. Always say please and thank you. Be a person who shows RESPECT to everyone. WOOF!

PATCHES SHARE DISCOVERY ADVENTURE
Be polite and always 'share' with others. Remember, if you 'share' with others then you 'care' for others.
Be a person who will always SHARE with others!

PATCHES NEXT TRAVEL QUEST ON JOURNEY THREE IS TAKING US TO PATCHES BIBLE MEMORY DISCOVERY ADVENTURE!

BUBBA SAYS: We have TRAVELED through '3' EXCITING PATCHES BIBLE DISCOVERY ADVENTURES on this JOURNEY!

BAILEE says: ARF! ARF We are having so much fun on BIBLE DISCOVERY ADVENTURES!

BUBBA SAYS: What BIBLE VERSES did we learn about on this JOURNEY TRAVELING through PATCHES BIBLE DISCOVERY ADVENTURES?

Can you remember the '3' PATCHES BIBLE DISCOVERY ADVENTURES in TRAVEL QUEST JOURNEY THREE?

Lets remember the '3' PATCHES BIBLE DISCOVERY ADVENTURES together! Our '3' PATCHES BIBLE DISCOVERY ADVENTURES were: ARF! ARF!

PATCHES COURAGE BIBLE DISCOVERY ADVENTURE
Be strong and courageous. Do not be afraid or terrified of them, for the Lord your God goes with you; he will never leave you nor forsake you. DEUTERONOMY 31:6

PATCHES RESPECT BIBLE DISCOVERY ADVENTURE
Each of you must RESPECT his mother and father, and you must observe my Sabbaths. I am the LORD your God. LEVITICUS 19:3'

PATCHES SHARE BIBLE DISCOVERY ADVENTURE
Be a SHARING person! And do not forget to do good and to share with others, for with such sacrifices God is pleased. HEBREWS 13:16

PATCHES DISCOVERY ADVENTURES
'MEMORY MAP QUEST THREE'

BAILEE SAYS: PATCHES, ARF! ARF! We are having so much fun on our BIBLE DISCOVERY ADVENTURES

PATCHES barks: WOOF! Our TRAVEL QUEST on JOURNEY THREE takes us to PATCHES DISCOVERY ADVENTURES MEMORY MAP QUEST THREE! Let's get started and use our MEMORY together! Fill in the missing words as we travel back through PATCHES DISCOVERY ADVENTURES JOURNEY THREE together.

Always have COURAGE and don't be afraid. Believe in yourself and you can accomplish anything. Always have _____ and don't be afraid. Believe in yourself and you could accomplish anything you try to do.
The missing word is COURAGE.

DEUTERONOMY 31:6 Be strong with COURAGE. Do not be afraid or terrified of them, for the Lord your God goes with you. Be strong with _____. Do not be afraid or terrified of them, for the Lord your God goes with you.
The missing word is COURAGE.

Be polite and show RESPECT for your parents and everyone. Always say please and thank you.. Be polite and show _____ for your parents and everyone. Always say please and thank you.. The missing word is RESPECT

LEVITICUS 19:3: Each of you must RESPECT his mother and father, and you must observe my Sabbaths. I am the LORD your God. Each of you must _____ his mother and father, and you must observe my Sabbaths.
I am the LORD your God. The missing word is RESPECT.

It is polite to always SHARE with others. So remember, if you SHARE with others then you 'care' for others. It is polite to always_____ with others. So remember, if you _____ with everyone then you 'care' for everyone.
The missing word is SHARE. WOOF!

HEBREWS 13:16: And do not forget to do good and to SHARE with others, for with such sacrifices God is pleased. And do not forget to do good and to _____ with others, for with such sacrifices God is pleased The missing word is SHARE.

WOOF! Great Job!

You have just earned PATCHES PIONEER PAW BADGE THREE! When you finish all '3' TRAVEL QUEST JOURNEYS with all '9' PATCHES DISCOVERY ADVENTURES. You can become a JUNIOR EXPLORER in PATCHES DISCOVERY ADVENTURES PAW PATROL!

CONGRATULATIONS! You have just completed all 3 TRAVEL QUEST JOURNEYS and all '9' PATCHES DISCOVERY ADVENTURES.

You are now a JUNIOR EXPLORER in PATCHES PAW PATROL!

You are now ready for more exciting PATCHES DISCOVERY ADVENTURES with PATCHES DISCOVERY ADVENTURES TRAVEL QUEST JOURNEY FOUR!

PATCHES
DISCOVERY ADVENTURES

PATCHES DISCOVERY ADVENTURES **JOURNEY FOUR**

PATCHES LOVE DISCOVERY ADVENTURE

PATCHES EQUALITY DISCOVERY ADVENTURE

PATCHES BE KIND DISCOVERY ADVENTURE

What exciting DISCOVERY ADVENTURE would you like to TRAVEL on with **PATCHES?**

PATCHES
DISCOVERY ADVENTURES

PATCHES EQUALITY DISCOVERY ADVENTURE
PATCHES POSITIVE DISCOVERY ADVENTURE
PATCHES LOYALTY DISCOVERY ADVENTURE
PATCHES PATIENCE DISCOVERY ADVENTURE
PATCHES BE KIND DISCOVERY ADVENTURE
PATCHES DISCIPLINE DISCOVERY ADVENTURE
PATCHES LOVE DISCOVERY ADVENTURE
PATCHES CHANGE DISCOVERY ADVENTURE
PATCHES COURTEOUS DISCOVERY ADVENTURE

Plus Many More PATCHES DISCOVERY ADVENTURES!

Come and join PATCHES on her next exciting DISCOVERY ADVENTURE JOURNEYS

What PATCHES DISCOVERY ADVENTURE would you like to go on with PATCHES next?

RANGER
ARMY

SECRET
MYSTERY
MILITARY
MISSIONS

AIRIAL
AIRFORCE

SECRET
MYSTERY
MILITARY
MISSIONS

PATCHES
EXPLORER
PATCHES
DISCOVERY
ADVENTURES

CAMO
MARINES

SECRET
MYSTERY
MILITARY
MISSIONS

GUNNER
NAVY

SECRET
MYSTERY
MILITARY
MISSIONS

Everyone Meet FLASH 4!

FLASH 4 are very special dogs. They are PATCHES from PATCHES DISCOVERY ADVENTURES 3 brothers and 1 sister (CAMO, GUNNER, RANGER and AIRIAL) and they were all 5 born together at the same time. They all have different patches of hair that make up their coat of characters. Their character patches are what make PATCHES and FLASH 4 who they are. Just like your character makes you who you are!

FLASH 4 has something incredible about them. Their different character patches on their hair FLASH to teach them the right thing to do every where they go! WOOF! While their sister PATCHES travels on her DISCOVERY ADVENTURES as an EXPLORER all of the FLASH 4 serve our country in the Military. RANGER is in the ARMY, CAMO is in the MARINES, GUNNER is in the NAVY and AIRIAL is in the AIRFORCE and they travel on SECRET MYSTERY MILITARY MISSIONS ARF! ARF Come and join FLASH 4 as they starts traveling on their EXCITING SECRET MYSTERY MILITARY MISSIONS

LET'S START FLASH 4'S SECRET MYSTERY MILITARY MISSIONS

GUNNER'S SECRET SAFETY MYSTERY MILITARY MISSION
GUNNER'S SECRET TRUST MYSTERY MILITARY MISSION
GUNNER'S SECRET GUIDANCE MYSTERY MILITARY MISSION
GUNNER'S SECRET MYSTERY MILITARY MISSION MAP QUEST

CAMO'S SECRET RULES MYSTERY MILITARY MISSIONS
CAMO'S SECRET AFRAID MYSTERY MILITARY MISSION
CAMO'S SECRET RESCUE MYSTERY MILITARY MISSION
CAMO'S SECRET MYSTERY MILITARY MISSION MAP QUEST

AIRIAL'S SECRET BE FAIR MYSTERY MILITARY MISSION
AIRIAL'S SECRET HELP MYSTERY MILITARY MISSION
AIRIAL'S SECRET DIRECTIONS MYSTERY MILITARY MISSION
AIRIAL'S SECRET MYSTERY MILITARY MISSION MAP QUEST

RANGER'S SECRET PRACTICE MYSTERY MILITARY MISSION
RANGER'S SECRET WORK MYSTERY MILITARY MISSION
RANGER'S SECRET CLEAN MYSTERY MILITARY MISSION
RANGER'S SECRET MYSTERY MILITARY MISSION MAP QUEST

Meet GUNNER!

GUNNER is in the NAVY NSWC Naval Special Warfare Group and he is a Navy Seal on Team 1 in Search of Classified Information to Solve SECRET MYSTERY MILITARY MISSIONS

"GUNNER" NAVY

4⁴²

Meet CAMO!

CAMO is in the USMC Special Forces and is a Marine Recon Operator in Search of Top Classified Information to Solve SECRET MYSTERY MILITARY MISSIONS

CAMO - MARINES

Meet AIRIAL!

AIRIAL is in the Airforce AFSOC Special Operations Command and she is a Ace Pilot in the 1ˢᵗ Special Operations Wing in Search of Classified Information to Solve SECRET MYSTERY MILITARY MISSIONS

' AIRIAL ' AIRFORCE

Meet RANGER!

RANGER is in the Army USASOC Special Operations Command and he is a Ranger in the 1st Special Forces Operations Delta in Search of Classified Information to Solve SECRET MYSTERY MILITARY MISSIONS

"RANGER" ARMY

Copyrighted @ 2014 by Vincent R Faulkner

All rights reserved. No part or portion of this publication or any portion of images or stories may be reproduced, electronically or mechanically transferred in any form or fashion such as print, media, digital, physical products stored in a retrieval systems, transmitted or used in any form or manner whatsoever without the exclusive express written legal permission of the author and publisher with the exception of the use of brief quotations or images in a book review or for promotions.

Created 2014
Printed in U.S.A
1ST Edition Printing 2014
Characters, Cover and Content by Author.

And you may contribute a verse
What will your verse be?

No Matter what people tell you,
Words and ideas can change the world!

FAULKNER PUBLISHING
The Legacy Continues

Vincent R Faulkner
Smyrna, Tennessee 37167

ADDITIONAL COPIES:
EBOOKSBYFAULKNER.COM
AMAZON.COM